SCHOLASTIC

LITERACY PLACE®

Information Finders

ISBN 0-439-06144-X

TABLE OF CONTENTS

Information Finders

THEME
Information comes
from many sources.

UNIT 5

Information Finders

Information Finders

THEME
Information comes from many sources.

UNIT 5

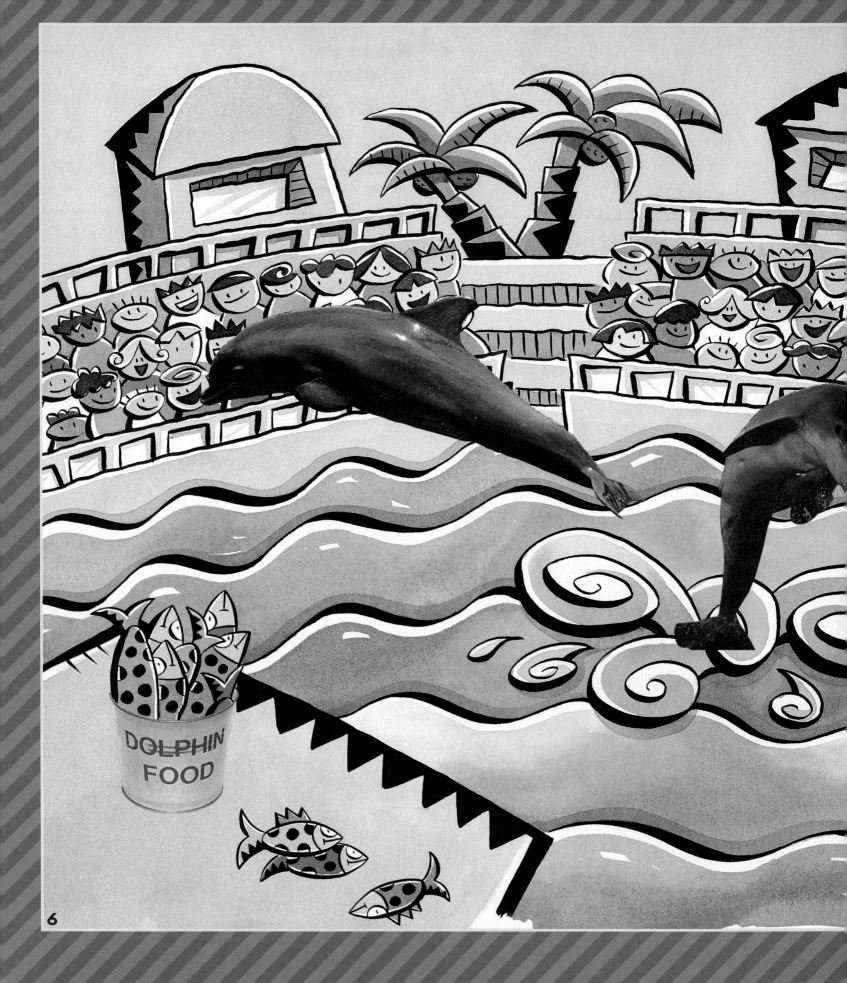

Welcome to

LITERACY PLACE

*Learn at
an Aquarium*

Information comes
from many sources.

One fish, two fish, three fish, more
Fish that dart and dip and slide

Fish that glide on fins like wings

Flat fish, round fish
A very long and thin fish

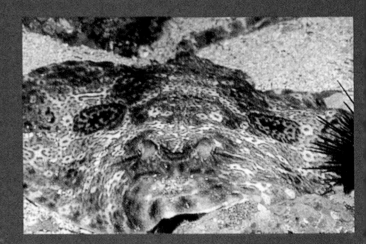

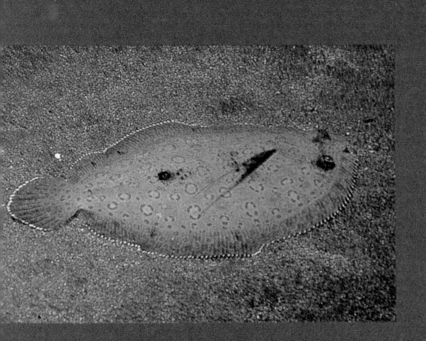

Spotted fish, dotted fish

Fish with lines and stripes and waves

Fish with mouths that open wide
Mouth like a tube, mouth like a beak
Mouth that belongs to a monster of the deep

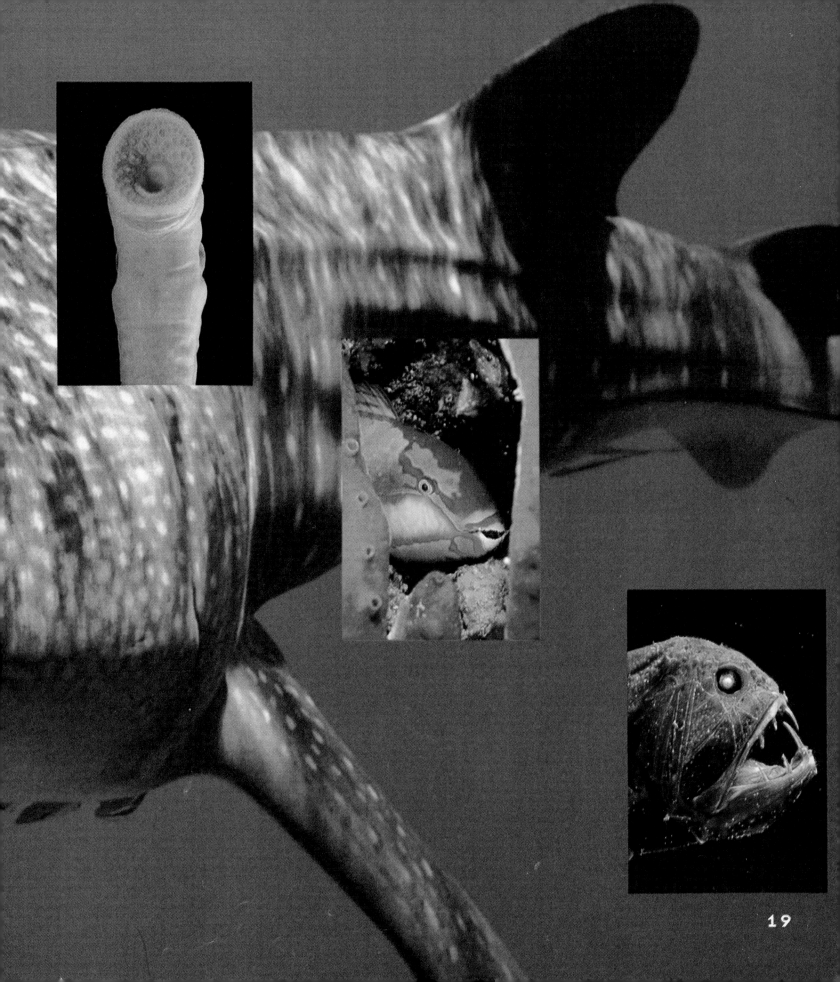

A long nose, a flat nose, a hard-to-ignore nose
A nose that looks like it could cut wood
A nose that shines in the dark!

Red eyes

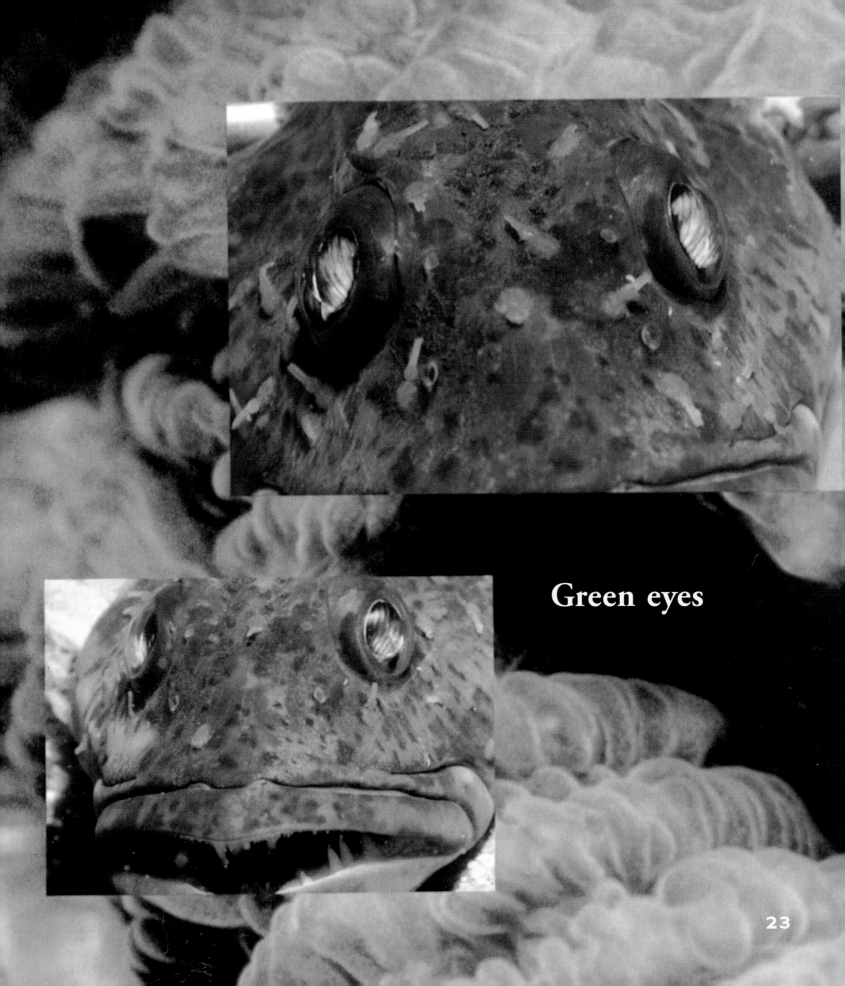

Green eyes

23

Great big pretend eyes

Eyes that are hooded

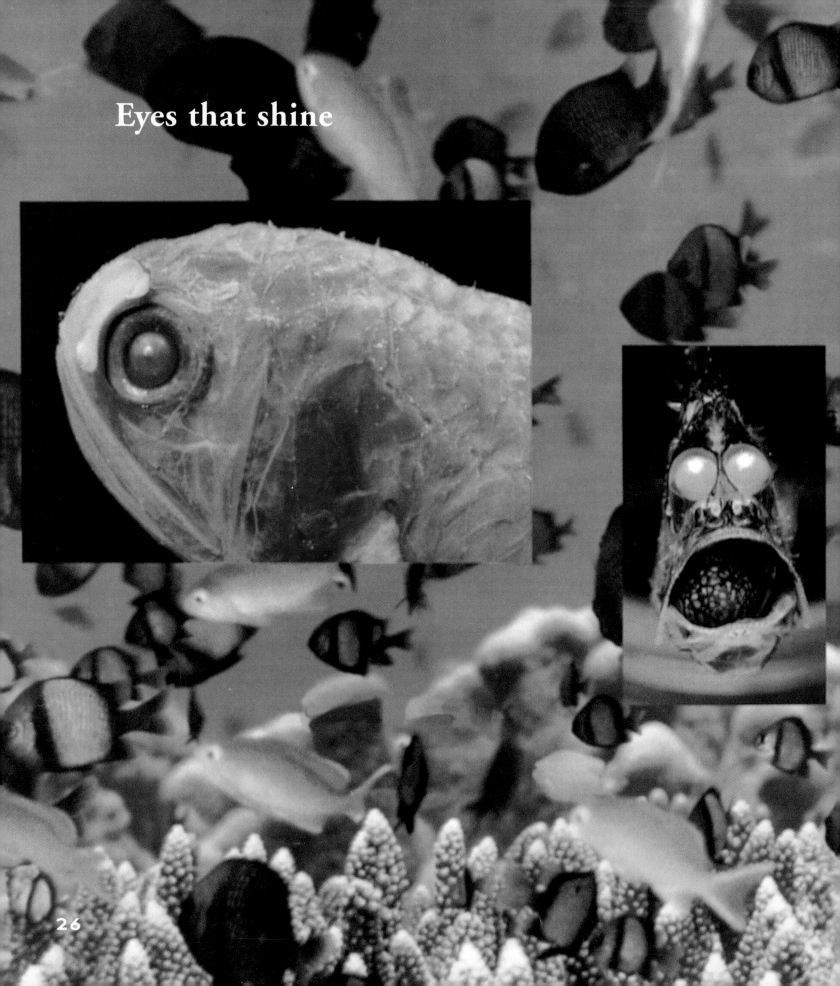

Eyes that shine

Eyes that stick up like periscopes

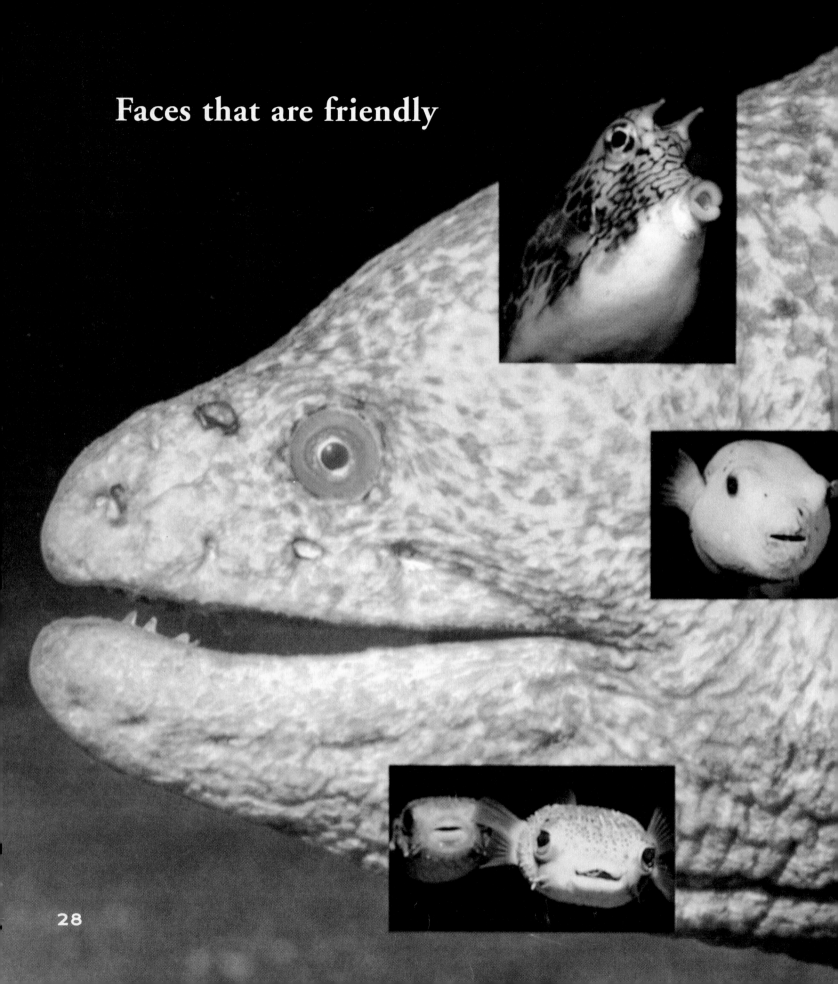

Faces that are friendly

28

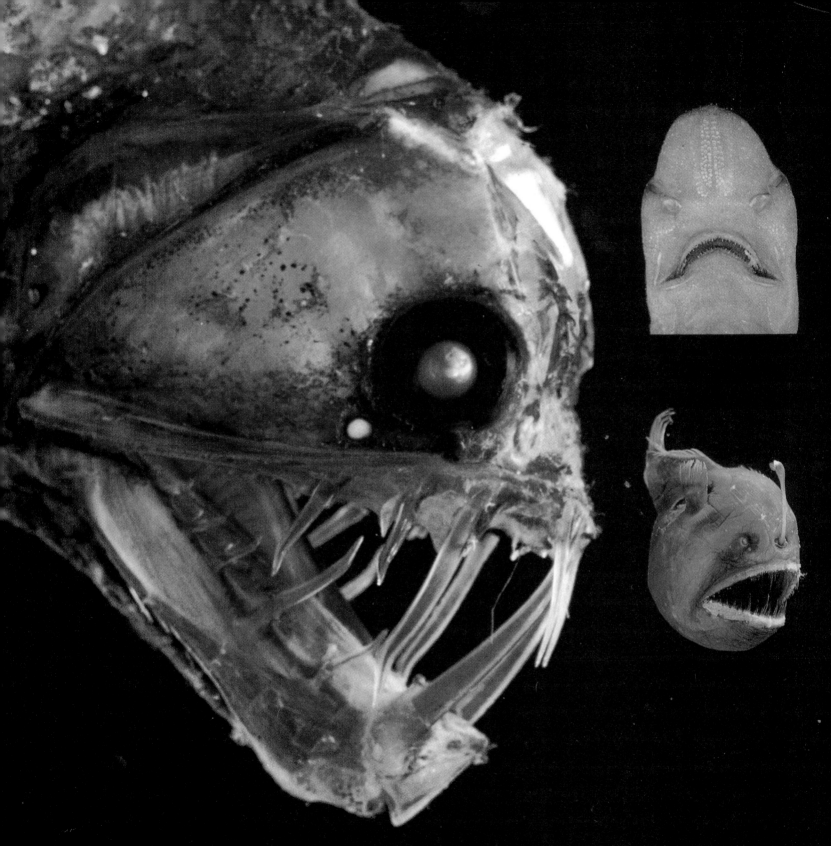

Faces that are fierce

Faces that could be sad or mad

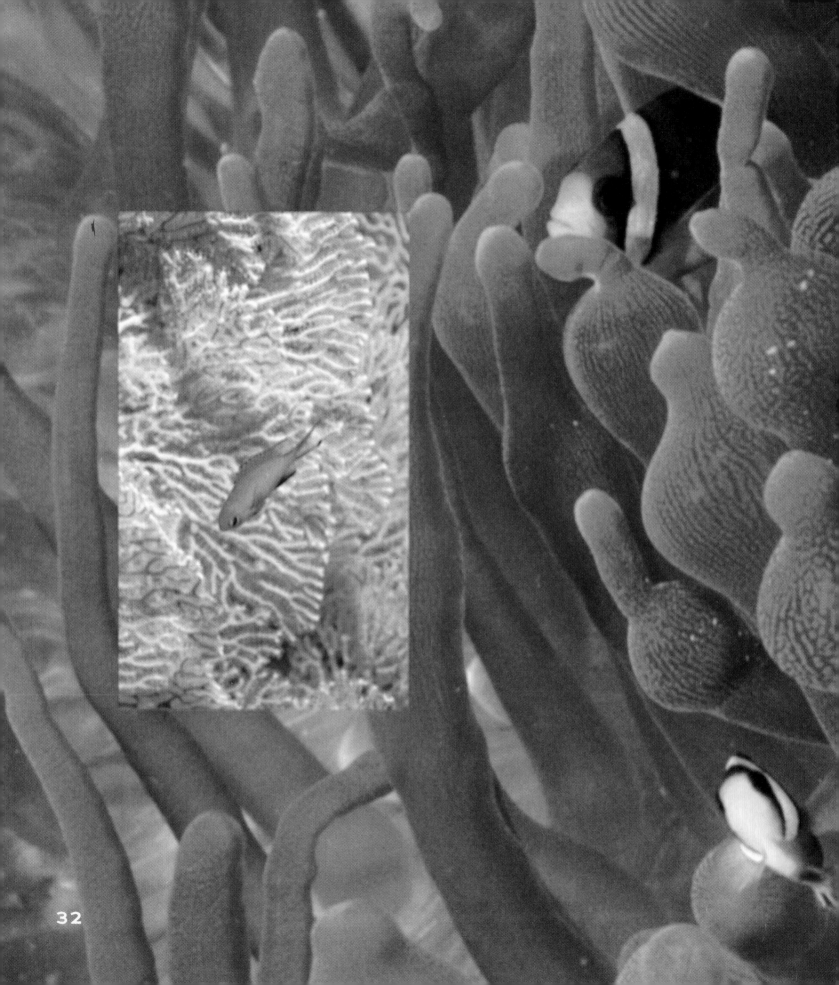

One fish, two fish, three fish, four
Deep in the ocean, there are thousands more!

 Read Together!

Laela Sayigh

Marine Biologist

Laela Sayigh studies dolphins. She wants to know how dolphins make sounds from their throats. Here's how she gathers and uses information at work.

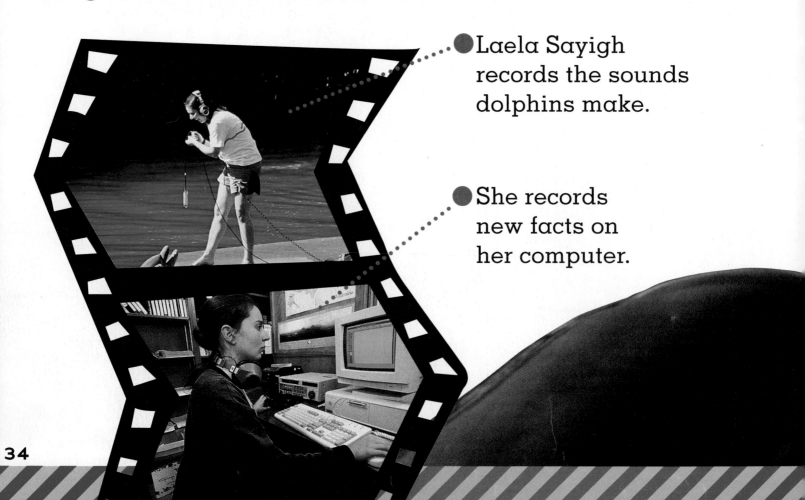

• Laela Sayigh records the sounds dolphins make.

• She records new facts on her computer.

Laela Sayigh
also writes
down what
she sees.

Think About Reading

1. What three different fish shapes does the story name?

2. Why are some fish noses hard to ignore?

3. Why do some fish have spikes and spines?

4. Why do you think <u>Fish Faces</u> shows photographs instead of drawings?

5. How is the author of <u>Fish Faces</u> like Laela Sayigh?

Write Labels

Fish Faces showed many different fish. Draw your own picture of a fish. Write labels on your picture to show the different parts of the fish. You may want to label the mouth, eye, fin, and tail.

Literature Circle

Talk about some ways the fish in Fish Faces are different from each other. Which fish do you think is the most unusual? Why?

Author
Norbert Wu

Wouldn't it be fun to take pictures under water? Norbert Wu thinks so. His job isn't all fun, though. Sometimes he is chased by sharks. He has even been run over by an iceberg! Still, Wu likes taking underwater photos and sharing them with other people.

More Books by Norbert Wu

- Life in the Ocean

- A City Under the Sea: Life in a Coral Reef

- Beneath the Waves: Exploring the Hidden World of the Kelp Forest

Hello Reader!
Level 1
SCIENCE
Preschool—Grade 1

I'm a Caterpillar

by Jean Marzollo
Illustrated by Judith Moffatt

SCHOLASTIC

Scholastic 0-590-84779-1/$3.50 US/$4.50 CAN

I'm a caterpillar.
Munch.
Crunch.

I'm getting bigger!
Munch.
Crunch.

Munch. Crunch.
Munch. Crunch.

That's it.
No more food.
I'm done.

It's time to hang from a stem.

I wait,
and wait,
and wait.

I shiver,
I twist.
I split my skin!

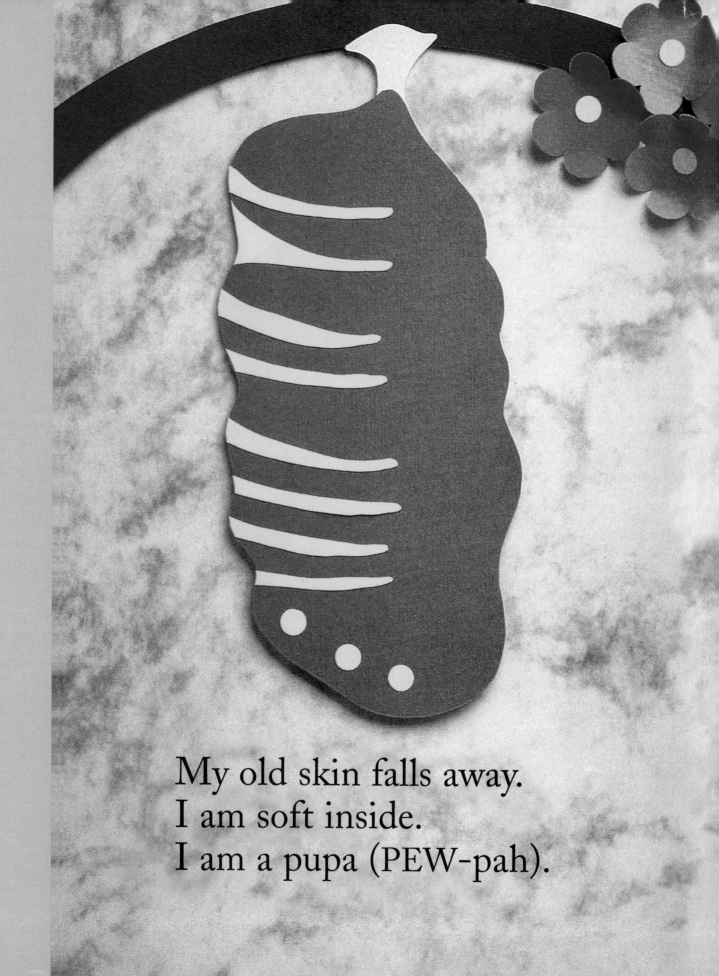

My old skin falls away.
I am soft inside.
I am a pupa (PEW-pah).

I grow a shell
to protect the pupa.
I am now a chrysalis
(KRIS-ah-lis).

48

I keep changing.
Soon I'll come out.
What will I be?

A butterfly!
Push.
Crack.
Wow!
I'm free!

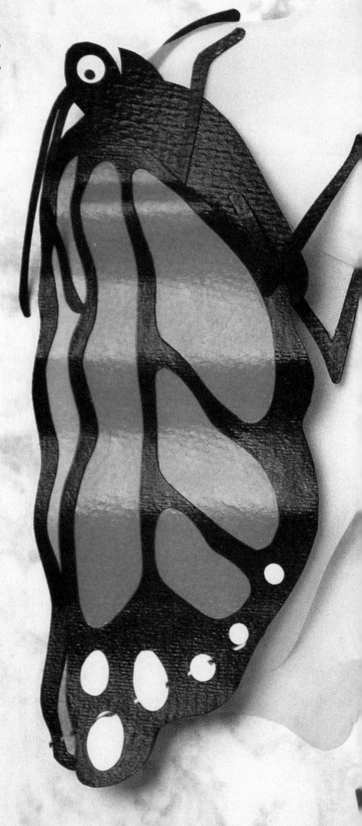

My wings are all wet.

My wings dry off.
They unfold.

Flap. Flap.
Hey!
I can fly!
Ta-da!

I visit flowers.
I drink nectar.
Yum!

My mouth is like
a straw.
Sip.
Sip.
Sip.

I have a mate.
We visit many flowers.

We're not afraid of birds.
They know that
we taste awful.

Soon I will lay my eggs.

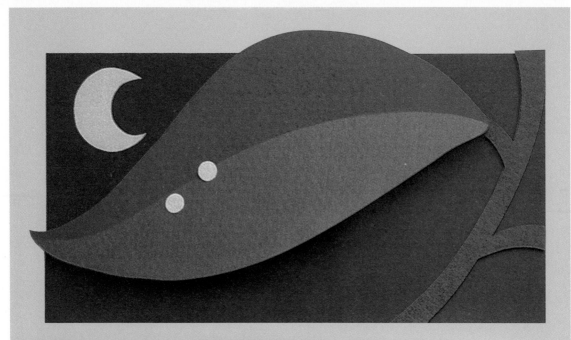

The eggs have thin shells.

Baby caterpillars crawl out.

Hi! I'm a caterpillar.

Munch. Crunch.

caterpillar

eggs

chrysalis

butterfly

What will happen
to me next?
Do you know?

Caterpillars

What do caterpillars do?
Nothing much but chew and chew.

What do caterpillars know?
Nothing much but how to grow.

They just eat what by and by
will make them be a butterfly,

But that is more than I can do
however much I chew and chew.

Aileen Fisher

67

Think About Reading

Finish the story map by answering the questions.
Write the answers on another piece of paper.

1.
What does a caterpillar turn into when it hangs upside down?

2.
What does it become next?

3.
What does the chrysalis become?

4.
What happens when the butterfly lays eggs?

Write Cartoon Dialogue

What do you think a caterpillar and a butterfly would say to each other? Draw a caterpillar and a butterfly on another piece of paper. Write words for both animals to say to each other.

Literature Circle

What if the caterpillar in I'm a Caterpillar could meet the poet who wrote "Caterpillars"? What might the caterpillar tell the poet? What might the poet tell the caterpillar?

Author
Jean Marzollo

Don't forget! That's good advice from Jean Marzollo. Marzollo knows that everyone has good ideas for writing. Still, it's easy to forget those good ideas. Then, when it's time to write, it can be hard to think up a good idea. That's why Marzollo writes down all her ideas right away.

More Books by Jean Marzollo

- I Am Fire
- Happy Birthday, Martin Luther King
- Football Friends

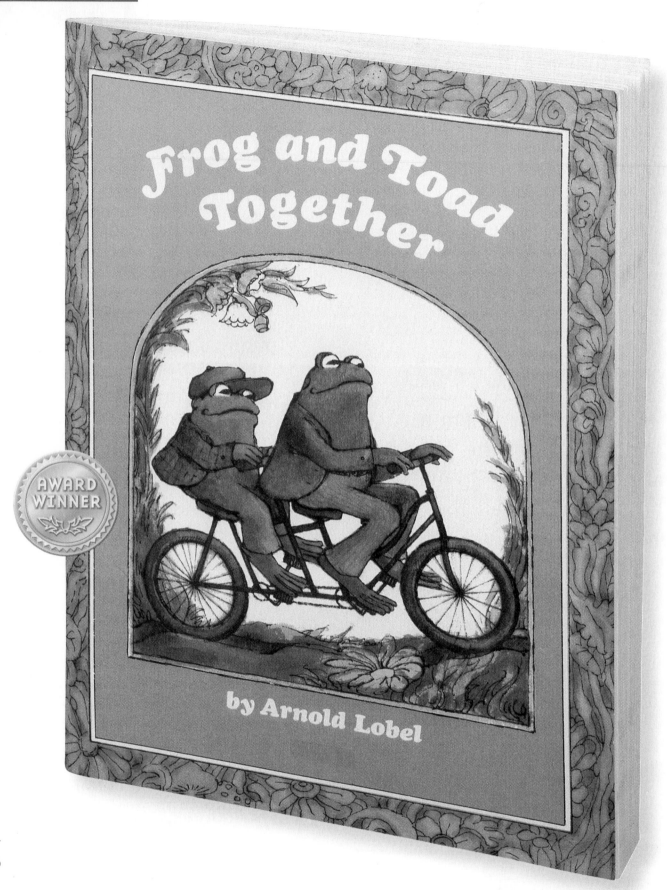

The Garden

Frog was in his garden.
Toad came walking by.
"What a fine garden
you have, Frog," he said.

"Yes," said Frog. "It is very nice,
but it was hard work."

"I wish I had a garden," said Toad.

"Here are some flower seeds.
Plant them in the ground," said Frog,
"and soon you will have a garden."

"How soon?" asked Toad.

"Quite soon," said Frog.

Toad ran home.
He planted the flower seeds.
"Now seeds," said Toad,
"start growing."
Toad walked up and down
a few times.
The seeds did not start to grow.

Toad put his head
close to the ground
and said loudly,
"Now seeds, start growing!"
Toad looked at the ground again.
The seeds did not start to grow.

Toad put his head
very close to the ground and shouted,
"NOW SEEDS, START GROWING!"

Frog came running up the path.
"What is all this noise?" he asked.

"My seeds will not grow," said Toad.

"You are shouting too much,"
said Frog. "These poor seeds
are afraid to grow."

"My seeds are afraid to grow?"
asked Toad.

"Of course," said Frog.
"Leave them alone for a few days.
Let the sun shine on them,
let the rain fall on them.
Soon your seeds will start to grow."

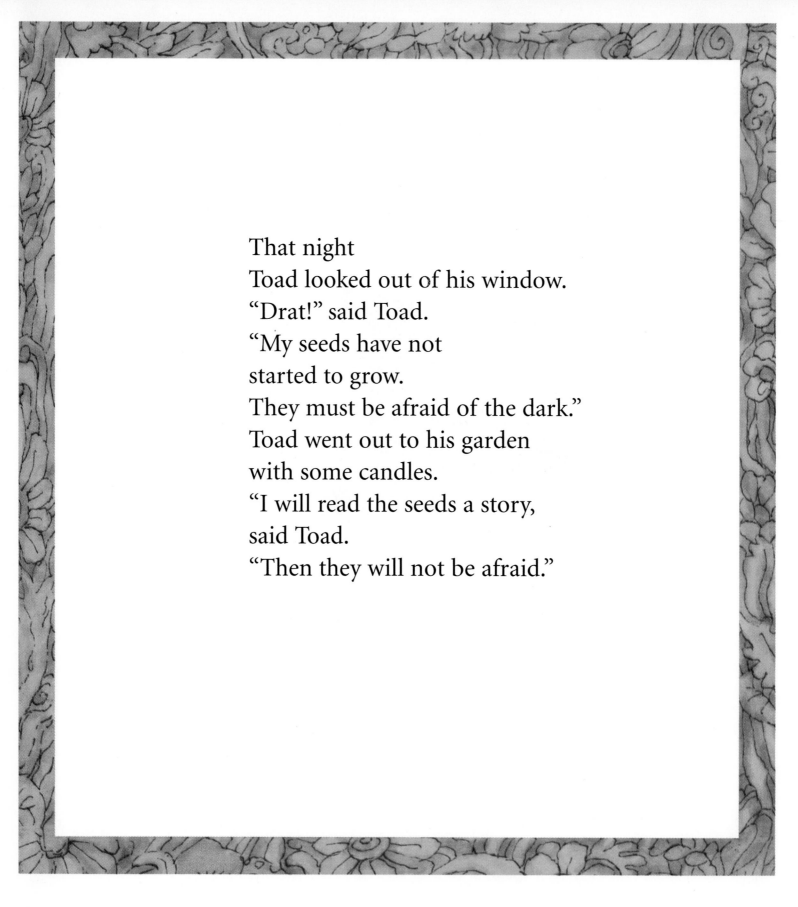

That night
Toad looked out of his window.
"Drat!" said Toad.
"My seeds have not
started to grow.
They must be afraid of the dark."
Toad went out to his garden
with some candles.
"I will read the seeds a story,
said Toad.
"Then they will not be afraid."

Toad read a long story
to his seeds.

All the next day
Toad sang songs
to his seeds.

And all the next day
Toad read poems
to his seeds.

And all the next day
Toad played music
for his seeds.

Toad looked at the ground.
The seeds still did not
start to grow.
"What shall I do?" cried Toad.
"These must be
the most frightened seeds
in the whole world!"

Then Toad felt very tired,
and he fell asleep.

"Toad, Toad, wake up," said Frog.
"Look at your garden!"
Toad looked at his garden.
Little green plants were coming up
out of the ground.

"At last," shouted Toad,
"my seeds have stopped
being afraid to grow!"

"And now you will have
a nice garden too," said Frog.

"Yes," said Toad,
"but you were right, Frog.
It was very hard work."

Tommy

by Gwendolyn Brooks

I put a seed into the ground.
And said, "I'll watch it grow."
I watered it and cared for it
As well as I could know.

One day I walked in my back yard,
And oh, what did I see!
My seed had popped itself right out,
Without consulting me.

Think About Reading

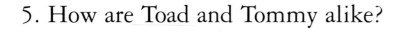

1. What does Toad wish?

2. Why does Toad shout at his seeds?

3. How do you think Toad feels while he waits for his seeds to grow?

4. What if Toad had not read and made music for his seeds? What do you think would have happened?

5. How are Toad and Tommy alike?

Write a Headline

Toad thinks his garden is big news! He wants to write a story for the newspaper about how to start a nice garden. Write a headline for Toad's news story. Your headline should be short and say something about the news story.

Literature Circle

Did you think "The Garden" was funny? Which parts of the story did you find funny? How did Toad's attitude toward the plants make the story funnier?

Author Arnold Lobel

Arnold Lobel believed artists and writers should use their own lives in their work. Lobel even used a picture of himself in one of his books. Don't look for a drawing of a man, though. Lobel drew himself as a pig—a pig with glasses and a mustache, working hard to draw a good picture.

More Books by Arnold Lobel

- Days With Frog and Toad
- Grasshopper on the Road
- Owl at Home

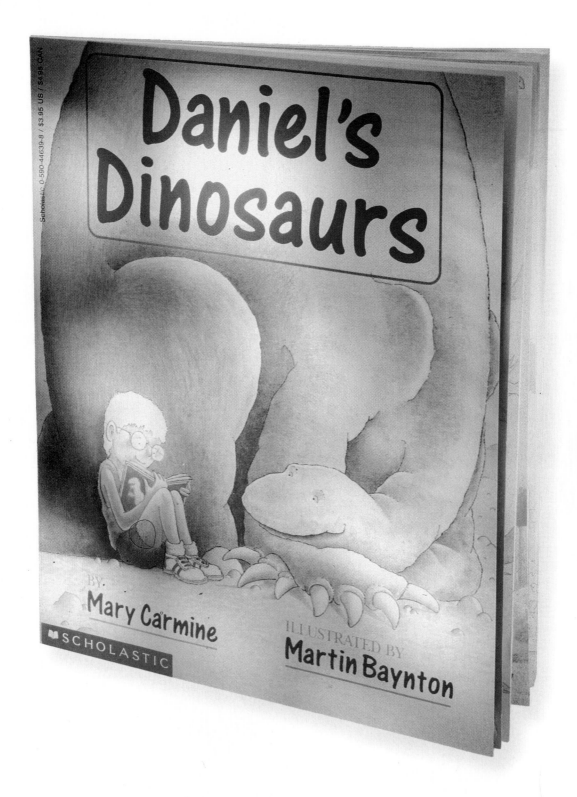

Scholastic 0-590-44639-8 / $3.95 US / $4.95 CAN

Daniel's Dinosaurs

BY
Mary Carmine

SCHOLASTIC

ILLUSTRATED BY
Martin Baynton

Daniel loved dinosaurs.
He loved big dinosaurs
and he loved little dinosaurs.

At the library,
he read books about dinosaurs.
When he drew pictures,
he drew pictures of dinosaurs.

When he wrote stories,
he wrote stories about dinosaurs.

Daniel's dinosaurs were everywhere.
Two Plateosaurs lived next door.

A Segnosaurus sat behind each check-out at the supermarket.

93

An Allosaurus directed traffic,
and one unknown variety barked at him
from behind a high fence every morning
as Daniel passed by on his way to school.

Daniel's teacher
was a nice, friendly, plant-eating Diplodocus,
but sometimes . . .

97

she turned into
a big, fierce Tyrannosaurus!

"I wish you'd think of something else sometimes,"
said Daniel's mother.
"Why don't we go to the city
and visit the Aquarium?"

"That's a good idea," said Daniel.
"I like fish . . .
but not as much as dinosaurs."

It was a long drive to the city.
All the way there,
Daniel drew pictures of dinosaurs.

A smiling Ceratosaurus took their money
at the ticket office.

Daniel and his mother looked at the rock pools,
the sea horses, and the little fish.

They looked at the stingrays . . .

and stayed for a long time.

They looked at the octopuses . . .

and stayed even longer.

Then they looked at the sharks . . .

106

and stayed for a very long time indeed.

As they left, Daniel said goodbye
to the smiling, grey nurse shark
in the ticket office . . .

from

I Can Read with My Eyes Shut!
By Dr. Seuss

The more that you read,

the more things you will know.

The more that you learn,

the more places you'll go.

Think About Reading

Think about Daniel's Dinosaurs. Finish the story map by writing each sentence on another piece of paper.

In the beginning, Daniel saw _____ everywhere.

↓

He saw two _____, a _____, an _____, and a _____.

↓

Then Daniel and his mother went to the _____.

↓

At the end, Daniel saw a _____ in the ticket office.

Write a Journal Entry

Maybe Daniel keeps a journal. He writes about the special things he sees and does. What do you think Daniel will add to his journal on the day he goes to the aquarium? Write Daniel's journal entry for this day.

Literature Circle

How would you describe Daniel to someone who hasn't read the story? Would you want to be like Daniel? Why or why not?

Author
Mary Carmine

Almost all children like to know about dinosaurs! Some parents check out dinosaur books from the library or look for dinosaur shows on TV. That's not what Mary Carmine did. When her son asked about dinosaurs, she wrote a book for him. That's right—Daniel's Dinosaurs!

THE PLANT CASTLE

by Pat Mora

illustrated by Gerardo Suzan

AWARD WINNER

SCHOLASTIC

Every day after school, I go to the arboretum. People come
from all around to see the plants and trees and flowers that
grow inside. My mother works there, studying the plants.
Today Beth, a new girl at my school, comes with me.

When we get to the arboretum, my mother meets us.
She says, "¿Cómo estás, Carmen?" and gives me a hug.
She says hello to Beth and Beth smiles. I think that Beth
feels shy.

"Beth, let's go to the desert," I say.

"The desert?" asks Beth.

Even when it's snowing outside, this room is always
dry and hot. It reminds me of the desert where my aunt
Nina lives.

I show Beth the cacti in the sunny desert room. These plants are called succulents because they store water in their leaves. Their sharp thorns keep away thirsty desert animals like mice and rabbits.

We read the names of the plants on the signs. Our favorites are the fishhook and pincushion cacti.

We go to the orchid house next. We see beautiful purple
and yellow and white flowers blooming on tree branches.
    We spot a butterfly. "Let's follow it!" I say.
    The butterfly flies into the room where my friends Sonia
and Mike are making a spring garden.

120

Beth and I bend down and watch a waterwheel turning by a tiny windmill. Sonia lets us dip our fingertips in the brook. We see a cottage that is just the right size for mice. We peek inside the small windows.

"There's the butterfly!" says Beth suddenly.

"Come on," I say. "It's going to the rain forest."

121

PALM TREE

BANANA TREE

We follow the butterfly into a room filled with tall green trees. The air feels heavy and wet in the rain forest room. We smell the leaves and flowers and hear a waterfall.

We cross a bridge. Beth looks down and calls, "Fish!" Orange and white fish are swimming in the clear water below us.

I look way up high for the butterfly. Vines and large leaves brush against the glass ceiling. The tall trees are like giant umbrellas that protect the plants on the forest floor from the sun and the rain.

RUBBER TREE

SHRIMP PLANT

PALM TREE

ELEPHANT EARS

CACAO TREE

Next we go to the tropical room. Beth looks at a plant called elephant ears. She laughs and says, "Carmen, I see green elephants."

I point to the shrimp plant and say, "I see pink shrimp!"

"Look! The butterfly!" says Beth very softly, and we watch it fly up into a palm tree.

"I'm getting hungry," I say. "Bananas, papayas, and other delicious fruits grow here."

Beth reads the label near the cacao tree. I tell Beth that chocolate comes from this tree. And the tree comes from Mexico, like my grandparents.

Just then the butterfly lands on Beth's shirt. She reaches for it, but it flies away. "It's shy like me," she says.

"It's time to go home now, girls," says Mother, joining us. "But I hope you'll come back soon, Beth!"

"Thank you, I will!" says Beth. "I can't wait to tell everybody at home about this place."

I don't think that Beth feels shy now.

127

When we drive away, Beth looks back at the arboretum
and says, "It's like a castle glowing in the night!"
I nod my head and smile.

from Children's Guide

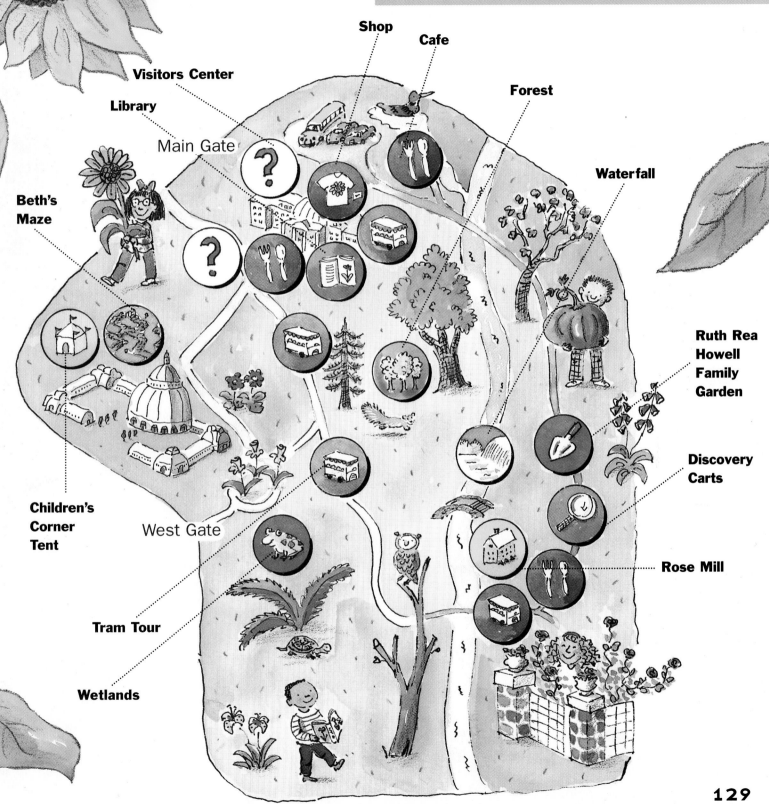

Shop

Cafe

Visitors Center

Forest

Library

Main Gate

Waterfall

Beth's
Maze

Ruth Rea
Howell
Family
Garden

Discovery
Carts

Children's
Corner
Tent

West Gate

Rose Mill

Tram Tour

Wetlands

Think About Reading

1. What does Carmen's mother do at the arboretum?

2. What kind of weather does a desert have?

3. How do you think the elephant ears plant got its name?

4. How can you tell that Beth had a good time at the arboretum?

5. How is the arboretum in <u>The Plant Castle</u> like the botanical garden in "Children's Guide"?

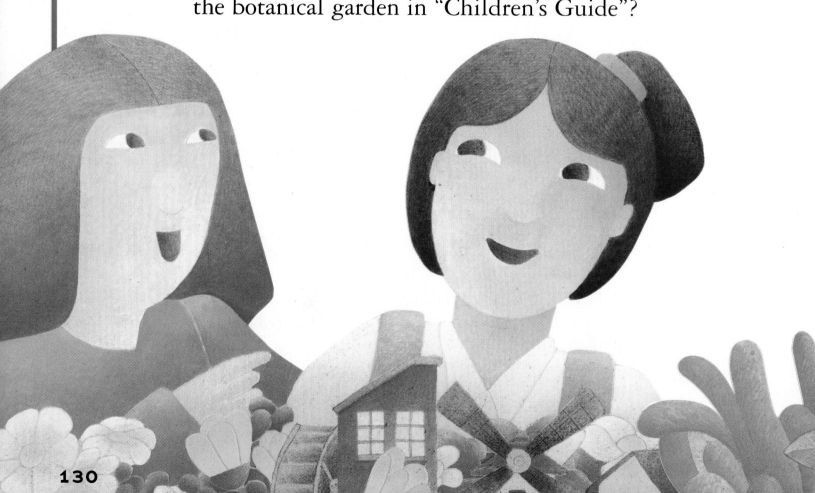

Write a Thank-You Letter

Beth had a great time at the arboretum! She would like to write Carmen a thank-you letter. In her letter, she wants to tell why she likes being at the arboretum. Write a thank-you letter for Beth to send Carmen.

Literature Circle

What if you could visit the New York Botanical Garden and the arboretum in The Plant Castle? What would you most want to see? Why? Talk about your ideas.

PLANT

AUTHOR
Pat Mora

Author Pat Mora says, "I'm lucky!" She's lucky because she grew up speaking two languages—English and Spanish. She's also lucky because she is a writer. All her life she has liked reading books. "Now I get to write them, too," she explains.

More Books by Pat Mora

- A Birthday Basket for Tia
- Tomas and the Library Lady
- The Desert Is My Mother/ El Desierto Es Mi Madre

You will find all your vocabulary words in ABC order in the Glossary. This page shows you how to use it.

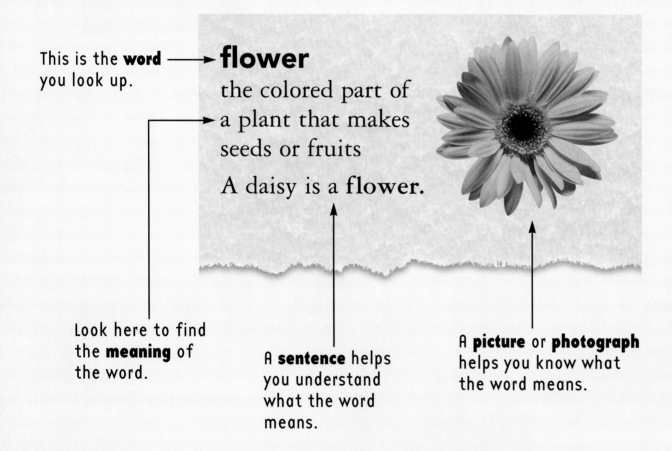

This is the **word** you look up.

flower
the colored part of a plant that makes seeds or fruits

A daisy is a **flower.**

Look here to find the **meaning** of the word.

A **sentence** helps you understand what the word means.

A **picture** or **photograph** helps you know what the word means.

butterfly

a flying insect with big wings, often in bright colors

The **butterfly** flew over the wall.

city

a large town where many people live and work

A **city** has tall buildings, lots of noise, and many busy people.

desert

a dry land with few plants

It is hot and dry in the **desert**.

desert

dry

to become free of wetness

Our wet clothes will **dry** in the sun.

eyes

the two parts of your face that you use to see with

I went to the doctor to have my **eyes** checked.

fins

small parts on a fish's body that flap to move it through water

Fins help a fish to swim.

fish

an animal with fins and scales that lives in water

A **fish** lives and breathes under water.

flower

the colored part of a plant that makes seeds or fruits

A daisy is a **flower**.

flower

forest

a big area full of trees and plants

We hiked on a trail through the **forest**.

frog

a small green or brown animal with webbed feet and long back legs

I saw a **frog** jump into the pond.

fruits

the part of plants that are juicy, fleshy, and have seeds

Oranges and bananas are **fruits**.

garden

a piece of ground where flowers, vegetables, or trees grow

We grow carrots in our **garden**.

grow

to get bigger or to cause something to get bigger

The kitten will **grow** into a big cat.

leaves

the flat, usually green parts of plants or trees that grow from branches

Some **leaves** fall from trees in autumn.

library

a room or building where books are kept

People can borrow books from the **library** to read at home.

mouth

the opening in your face through which you take food

My teeth are in my **mouth**.

munch

to chew with a crunching sound

I heard my dog **munch** his hard food.

nose

the part of your face that you use to smell and to breathe

My **nose** is below my eyes and above my mouth.

office

a room or a building in which people work, usually at desks

Mom's computer is in her **office**.

plant

to put a plant or a seed in the ground and help it grow

Dad will **plant** grass in our yard.

seeds

small parts of plants from which new plants can grow

Tiny **seeds** can grow into trees.

shark

a kind of fish with sharp teeth that eats meat

I saw a large **shark** swimming in a huge tank.

straw

a hollow plastic or paper tube to drink through

Lee always drinks his juice through a **straw.**

supermarket

a large store that sells food and other things

My dad buys grapes, soap, and film at the **supermarket.**

supermarket

teacher

a person who shares knowledge and shows people how to do things

Our **teacher** told us how to add the numbers.

trees

large woody plants with trunks, roots, branches, and leaves

Apples grow on **trees.**

tree

wait

to stay or do nothing until something happens

We **wait** for the bus to come.

waves

curved, or up and down lines

Kerry used different colors to paint **waves** in her picture.

wet

covered with water or other liquid

The streets are **wet** on rainy days.

work

the effort to get something done

Moving rocks takes **work.**

Acknowledgments

Grateful acknowledgment is made to the following sources for permission to reprint from previously published material. The publisher has made diligent efforts to trace the ownership of all copyrighted material in this volume and believes that all necessary permissions have been secured. If any errors or omissions have inadvertently been made, proper corrections will gladly be made in future editions.

Table of Contents: From DANIEL'S DINOSAURS by Mary Carmine, illustrated by Martin Baynton. Illustrations copyright © 1990 by Martin Baynton. Reprinted by permission of Ashton Scholastic Ltd., New Zealand.

"Fish Faces" from FISH FACES by Norbert Wu. Copyright © 1993 by Norbert Wu. Reprinted by permission of Henry Holt and Co.

"I'm a Caterpillar" from I'M A CATERPILLAR by Jean Marzollo. Text copyright © 1997 by Jean Marzollo. Illustrations copyright © 1997 by Judith Moffat. Reprinted by permission of Scholastic Inc.

"Caterpillars" from CRICKET IN A THICKET by Aileen Fisher. Copyright © 1963 by Aileen Fisher. Copyright renewed © 1991 by Aileen Fisher. Used by permission of Marian Reiner for the author.

"Frog and Toad Together: 'The Garden'" from FROG AND TOAD TOGETHER by Arnold Lobel. Copyright © 1971 by Arnold Lobel. Reprinted by permission of HarperCollins Publishers.

"Tommy" from BRONZEVILLE BOYS AND GIRLS by Gwendolyn Brooks. Copyright © 1956 by Gwendolyn Brooks Blakely. Reprinted by permission of HarperCollins Children's Books, a division of HarperCollins Publishers.

"Daniel's Dinosaurs" from DANIEL'S DINOSAURS by Mary Carmine, illustrated by Martin Baynton. Text copyright © 1990 by Mary Carmine. Illustrations copyright © 1990 by Martin Baynton. Reprinted by permission of Ashton Scholastic Ltd., New Zealand.

"I Can Read With My Eyes Shut" from I CAN READ WITH MY EYES SHUT by Dr. Seuss. TM and copyright © 1978 by Dr. Seuss Enterprises, L.P. Reprinted by permission of Random House, Inc.

"The Plant Castle" from THE PLANT CASTLE by Pat Mora, illustrated by Gerardo Suzan. Copyright © 1996 by Scholastic Inc.

Photography and Illustration Credits

Photos: pp.6tl, 6mr, © Gerard Lacz/Animals Animals; pp.7br, 34br, 34tl, Maryellen Baker for Scholastic Inc.; p.35bl, Chip Henderson for Scholastic Inc.; pp.36–37, © Ron Dalquist/Superstock; pp.36br, 37br, 37c, © Norbert Wu; p.69, © Ellen Warner; p.85, Harper Collins; p.113, Courtesy Scholastic New Zealand; p.131, © Valerie Santiago; p.132br, © David Young Wolff/Tony Stone Images; p.135br, © Michael P. Gadomski/ PhotoResearchers.

Cover: Fred Bavendan/Minden Pictures

Back Cover: R.Faris/Corbis

Illustrations: pp.4–5:Karen Barbour for Scholastic Inc. pp.6–7: Jackie Snider. pp.82–83:Tungwai Chau for Scholastic Inc. pp.67–68:Doran Potka for Scholastic Inc. p.129:Paul Miesel for Scholastic Inc. p.130:Gerard Suzan

Illustrated Author Photos: pp.37, 69, 85, 113, 131: David Franck for Scholastic Inc.